To Gemma, Mia and Olly. Thanks for all your fintastic help and support.
Love you more than all the water in Atlantica.
Chris/Dad x

John, huge thanks for working with me on the book, it's been great fun.

Written by Chris Dehnert
Illustrated by John Elson

In partnership with XcelAthletic.com sportswear
& FootySchool.com soccer schools

Published by Banananas Publishing

Printed by Book Printing UK www.bookprintinguk.com
Remus House, Coltsfoot Drive, Peterborough, PE2 9BF
Printed in Great Britain

ISBN 978-1-0369-0160-8

Sharky's Soccer School

written by Chris Dehnert and
illustrated by John Elson.

In the bustling underwater city of Atlantica, Ruby, Billy, Thiago and Megan, known to everyone as the Sharky's, dreamt of one day becoming Atlantica's soccer champions!

To see how the Sharky's get on let's dive deep into the ocean and meet these talented, some would say fintastic, soccer Sharky's...

Ruby has dazzling skills,
she really is lightning quick.
Ruby glimmers through the ocean,
and has a tremendously good kick!

Billy, brave and determined,
he's a great big towering wall.
Billy uses all his might and fight,
to save the swirling ball!

Thiago loves to glide and tackle,
he never stops trying.
Win, lose or draw,
Thiago is never sighing.

Megan has ferocious shots,
scoring is her quest.
Megan locks in her target,
she is certainly one of the best!

Could it be their time to shine?
The cup final was fast approaching.
The Sharky's need to keep training,
with the help of some fantastic coaching!

The Sharky's have lots to do,
plenty to sink their teeth into!
Pass after pass, hour after hour,
hungry for the ball, ready to devour!

However the Sharky's path to success,
might not go entirely their own way.
Ramos and the Rams,
always like to have a say!

The Rams nudge, splish and splash,
bumping into everyone they see.
The Sharky's must play their own game,
and be the best that they can be!

It's the final, Sharky's versus Rams,
who will win by the end of this story?
Teamwork against slippery trickery,
only one team can grab the glory!

1-0 to the Rams early on,
they had a speedy start.
The Sharky's need to relax, keep on playing,
can they pick the Rams apart?

One, two, three goals were scored,
Ruby, twisting and turning,
the stadium roared!

Billy in goal, saving plenty of shots,
this Sharky was making some
incredible blocks!

Thiago darting all over the pitch,
with all his hard work he was getting a stitch!

Megan smashing goals in for fun,
finally it looked like...the Rams were done!

Hip hip hooray, songs were sung,
the Sharky's had only gone on...and won

They proved that with practice and teamwork,
dreams can be achieved.

Everyone kept on going, but most importantly,
they always believed.

It's time to say farewell,
there will be another game in a little while.
The Sharky's had lots of fun,
playing the game as it should be...

with a great big smile.

For their next adventure,
the Sharky's will travel far and wide.
Schooling everyone in the ocean,
no matter the tide.

Improving all sea creatures,
helping them join new teams.
Showing anyone in the water,
that you can make your own dreams!

See you all soon in our next soccer adventure!

Printed in Great Britain
by Amazon

51703582R00016